BROKEN GEMS

By Dr. Erica Kelly

BROKEN GEMS

It's time for restoration. You CAN be whole again!

No part of this publication may be reproduced in whole or in part, stored in a retrieval system, or transmitted in any form or by any means whether auditory, graphic, mechanical, electronic, or otherwise, without written permission of the author. Unauthorized reproduction of any part of this work is illegal and is punishable by law.

This book contains ideas and opinions of the author. The intention of this book is to provide information, helpful content, and motivation to readers about the subjects addressed, however it is not meant as a substitute for direct expert assistance. If such level of assistance is required, the services of a competent professional should be sought. Although every precaution has been taken to verify the accuracy of the information contained herein, the author and publisher assume no responsibility for any errors or omissions.

No guarantees are expressed or implied by the author's choice to include any of the content in this volume. The author shall not be liable for any physical, psychological, emotional, financial damages. The reader is responsible for their own choices, actions, and results.

Copyright © 2022 Dr. Erica Kelly— All rights reserved
Cover design by LaolanArt
Author photo by Elle Harris Studios

ISBN 978-1-955727-14-3 (Paperback)
ISBN 978-1-955727-15-0 (Hardback)
ISBN 978-1-955727-20-4 (Digital)

Published by RIA JAY Publishing
3355 Lenox Road Suite 750 Atlanta, GA 30326
www.riajay.com

Printed in the United States of America First printing May 2022

Dedication

This book is dedicated to those who have shared their perspectives and truths about the battles and hurts that they've faced in their past and in society. Through their vantage point, I hope to shed light on a frustrated generation of men struggling to overcome and tackle obstacles designed to demolish them.

This book will allow men from all walks of life to explore and unearth their brokenness, as well as learn how to heal from their past traumas. Ultimately, the purpose is to bring strength, awareness, empowerment, knowledge, understanding, hope, and a renewed sense of self-worth. With a newfound wisdom, men will unveil their aspirations and will be provided the opportunity to thrive. Bearing in mind the impossible paradox of life, this book will implant a growth and renewed mindset in us all.

With love,
Dr. Erica Kelly

TABLE OF CONTENTS

INTRODUCTION..9

CHAPTER ONE: THE BUDDING STAGE
THE SEED...11
THE UNSPOKEN AND HIDDEN ABUSE...............................18
THE PREMISE..22

CHAPTER TWO: CONTROL HIS THINKING, OWN HIS ACTIONS
YOU CANNOT HIT BACK..26
PERMISSION NOT GRANTED: MAN UP!..............................32

CHAPTER THREE: UNHINGED
THE WORLD ON YOUR SHOULDERS....................................36
ECONOMIC CONFINES..40
WHO'S TO BLAME?..44

Chapter Four: Hard as Penitentiary Steel

How the Cards Were Dealt 50

Incoming Call | Raymond's Story 52

Captivity and Bondage | Daniel's Story 59

Point Blank Range | Nikko's Story 70

Struggle of the Captive Soul | Mont's Story 75

Found in the Grave | Tre's Story 86

Chapter Five: Solitaire Confinement of the Mind

Prepare for the Flood 90

Why? 94

The Flip Flop 103

The Educator's Guidance 107

Investment 112

Empowerment 117

Restored 119

INTRODUCTION

Transition is a word that can be easily interchanged with the terms evolution or transformation. During the transitional phase, you must make the adjustment from immaturity to maturity. Don't get masculinity confused with maturity. Just because you look like a man doesn't mean that you aren't shielding the little boy inside of you. This level of transformation is formulated from mindset growth instead of physical growth. If you do not allow room for mental development, change cannot take place. There must be a conscious sense of understanding and acceptance to acquire true transformation. This phase does not come with a set of instructions, nor a blueprint, but instead it is unique to each individual person.

Through the next chapters you'll explore hurts buried deep inside and how to unravel them. It won't be a smooth path, but it will be worth it. Though these pages will act as a guide, there is not a mistake-proof book to life. Just remember to plant one

> **When shifts and transitions in life shake you to the core, see that as a sign of greatness that's about to occur.** – *Anonymous*

hand in God's palm while keeping one foot in the world. This will help you to be led by faith as well as make you aware of issues that are affecting you. This will be a journey that will lead you to the truest and purest form of yourself and help you discover how great you really are.

Chapter ONE

The budding stage

The Seed

Despite humble beginnings, it's impossible to know our end. Our very existence starts as a small, feeble seed. Powerless at first but has the potential of obtaining extraordinary growth and undying strength. Many factors and influences aid the growth of this seed, molding us into who we will become. In this initial stage, watering, sunlight, fresh air, and good soil is crucial for developing deep, strong roots. Just the same, the seed can wither from lack of water, shrivel when light is dimmed, suffocate from lack of oxygen, and never root properly due to contaminated soil. This seed is you.

This seed was a miracle formed in the depths of your mother's belly as her body unconsciously protected you at all costs. This seed manifested into your presence. It was spawn, positioned, then orchestrated between man and woman where desire and love were uniquely intertwined. An immense level of importance was attached to the tiny seed from the moment of insemination. It had everything it needed for a healthy transition into this world... everything that it needed to flourish brilliantly. But what happens when this seed arrives to a place where its development and growth is halted? Now, the seeds fate is decided by the nourishment of others. These influences start with the same two people that made you, and they pose a very powerful impact. If they are careless and inconsistent in the way that they nurture you, this can change the trajectory of your life.

Most parents, despite their financial situations or personal circumstances, try their best when raising a child. They try to provide all the love, support, guidance, and care needed so that their child can have the best possible future. Of course, there is no handbook

> **Although it is the smallest of all seeds, when it is fully grown it is larger than the garden plants and becomes a tree, and the birds in the sky come and nest in its branches.** — *Matthew13:32*

on parenting, so the process is learn-as-you-go. Though love is given, sometimes it's the smallest things that can damage the seed. This can very well come by way of what we know as discipline or punishment. Sometimes, the harsh words and punishments may be too much for the seed in this delicate growth stage. You may have been told that strength is not possible without discomfort and experiencing a certain level of hurt. You may have been told to toughen up or not to cry. You may have been told that children are to be seen and not heard. You may have even been made to feel that your voice is insignificant, and your childhood gripes aren't "real problems." But as a child, you instinctively love your parents despite their flaws, absence, lack of love or harsh words. They are all you know. They are your protective shield, and you have pure delight in their presence even when your voice is shrouded, and your feelings are put aside.

After a while fear creep in, and you do everything to please your parents, but to what expense? You learn to shut your mouth and do whatever they say. You learn to toughen up and not cry. You learn to "grow up" and set aside your childish ways even though you have many years left before adulthood. You learn that these things are the norm, even though they are too much for the young seed to bear. The truth is your parents, like most parents, stifled your freedom of expression. They shut out your voice in the same way their parents shut out their voice. It's a vicious cycle and when continued, we continue to create stunted seeds and broken gems. Though your parents may have set out to make you be filled with love, hope, integrity, and strength, like a sponge, you absorbed everything poured into you; the good and the bad. What was poured in you at the seed stage may be the reason for your problems during your growth stage and beyond.

Soon you are sprouting into a young man, figuring out life as it comes to you. This phase is challenging. You try to become rooted in life, but the soil you were planted in as a seed did not nourish you properly. You didn't receive all the sunshine and love that you should have. Maybe you weren't watered or given the attention that a young child requires. All these things can impede on you in the budding phase. Trouble in school, focusing on goals, committing to relationships, and being dedicated to jobs may all be a direct effect from an undernourished seedling. Misguided and misunderstood, you lean on your own young knowledge to fix your situations, but this is only trial and error. It's not the doing in your current state, but the undoing of your past hurts and manipulations. Though at this age you may not know how to do this, at any stage in life you can look back and address childhood issues head-on. Healing is a process; it's never too late. Though you are no longer a seed, you are a plant who's constantly growing. It's up to you to uproot yourself and find a new home in nutrient rich soil.

Every so often, adults get lost in regret while thinking I wish I did this, or I wish I did that. You may have thought this, just as your parents have thought this, as well as many generations that came before you. Here's that vicious cycle again, but we must understand that we can't rewind time. The real deal is that everyone, no matter their age, sex, creed, or color is figuring it out as they go. You *will* make mistakes. You *will* fall down. You *will* get hurt. These things are inevitable. These may be disturbing facts, but it's true. Once we come to this realization, it helps us prepare for these hurdles in life and learn how to deal with them.

> **You look at me and cry; everything hurts. I hold you and whisper: but everything can heal.** — *Rupi Kaur*

Even the most knowledgeable person in the world doesn't know everything, just as the most loving person in the world sometimes fail to love. Therefore, the answer is not figuring it out, but learning to deal with our circumstances and heal from our past. Though you may see trials and dead ends, you are not alone. It's time to acknowledge your strength and face your issues. It's time to let your voice be heard in a world that is way too loud and infiltrated with not only the impressions of your parents, but of your peers, media, and anything else that has been stunting your growth.

Mediocracy may have set in, and you are getting use to the life you have. You stop fighting for dreams because they appear to be just that, a dream. You feel that you are fighting against the dry, atypical, unkempt terrain and you may not know how to replant yourself. In a life so challenging, you lose sight of the attainable victories, but guess what, YOU... CAN... WIN! Agony and let down creates a certain level of weakness, but don't get overwhelmed by distress. Sometimes it's our weakest moments where we find strength and discover deeper levels of self. So, keep grinding away at the things pressing against your expansion. Even though you may have been dropped at the wayside as a seedling, you can still grow expeditiously.

Now that you understand the challenges placed in front of you, are you ready to take a leap of faith? Are you ready to tap into the unused portion of your spiritual, psychological, and emotional consciousness? This realization begins in the mind, but so does the start of defeat. This part is like a double-edged sword... which side will you choose? The side of despair or the side of hope and promise?

Do not allow abandonment, lack of knowledge, or fear to be your excuse. Rising above the challenges will propel you to be an example for other men like yourself who is struggling to find their place in this life. It's time to break the cycle. Legitimate hard work and dedication will set you apart and help you to blossom. This will provide an exciting, new growth pattern for not only yourself, but for others. Do not allow your past to cripple you. Instead, lean on your past for understanding and learn to grow from it. As you conquer new goals and rid yourself of debilitating beliefs, you will attain a better understanding of self and maximize your strengths in each opportunity that life presents. Time to dig deep and get to work!

The unspoken and hidden abuse

Raising a child is one of the hardest, yet most gratifying things that someone can do. Think about it. A parent can mold and influence this tiny human being that knows nothing. Of course, there will be outside influences, but the core impact comes from the mother and father. No matter how great and loving, or no matter how abusive and manipulative a parent can be, that child will look to them for guidance because that's all they know.

Far too often we hear of cases where a child was badly beaten or sexually abused. These incidents commonly surround us in our own families, and more so, sometimes these children were us. Usually, parents do what they think is best for their children by protecting and guiding them. But what about the not-so-good parents? The parent that will curse you out and beat you in a drunken rage. The parent that will leave you home alone with no food to eat while they were on a three-day-high. The parent that allowed so many partners to come in and out of the house that you never knew who would be sitting on the couch as you fixed cereal in the morning. What about those parents?

These types of parents had their own struggles and were fighting their own battles. They were seeking love, acceptance, and a way to overcome their own neglect and heartbreak. Unfortunately, their temporary healings came at your expense. At the end of their displaced aggression, you may have experienced demoralizing, disheartening, and debilitating levels of abuse. As a child, you may not have seen this for what it was, but as you grew, you realized that life wasn't supposed to be that way. You started to pay attention with honed sight, while adjusting to your surroundings. You came to a place of acceptance. Although you knew the abuse was wrong, there was nothing more you could do. This is the person that is providing for you, caring for you, putting a roof over your head and food in your mouth. So, you shut up. You don't complain. You wait out your 18 years like a jail sentence and promise to move out as soon as you're legal. You wait… and take it. You don't cry because, well, boys can't cry, so you internalize it. You can't escape mentally or physically, and you can't hit back. When you do speak up in defense, you are considered disrespectful and ungrateful. There is no escaping this tyrant that you call a parent, so you endure.

Recollections of the pain are hitting on a deeper level. No matter the amount of success you reach, social status you obtain, or money you earn, you just can't shake what has happened to you as a child. In the eyes of everyone else, you are a stand-up man. You are confident and secure in yourself and can't be shook. But it's difficult for even the most solid people to stand solo in the face of hostility and discomfort. You *need* support. You *need* healing. You *need* release. You need these things because you are like a volcano ready to erupt. A volcano can be dormant for many years before spewing its hot lava and destroying everything in its path. You don't want to be this volcano. You don't want to destroy and hurt people in your path. You must learn to release on your own accord to avoid this type of spontaneous eruption.

> **The greater a child's terror, and the earlier it is experienced, the harder it becomes to develop a strong and healthy sense of self.** – *Nathaniel Branden,*

Acknowledging and sharing your story will not only help you, but it will also help others around you. People in similar situations will be able to relate, release, heal and grow. Confession is your opportunity to free yourself from bondage.

The road to healing is not easy. You may be overwhelmed with thoughts of how everyone will view you once your inner secrets are revealed. Doubts and confusion flood your mind when you think of the outcome. Will your family believe you? Will they sweep your feelings under the rug? Will they scorn you after telling the family secret? No matter the outcome, it's time to set the captives free. This truth is about to launch you into manhood. By verbalizing your hurts and no longer suppressing information about what you have suffered, you can relieve yourself of its ownership. Let that thing go! It is no longer your life. Though it happened, it doesn't need to live within you. Evict that hurt from its home. It is no longer welcome in your temple.

The premise

Single parenthood is known to carry over from one generation to the next. Those who are single parents due to unplanned or teenage pregnancies know all-to-well the struggles and sacrifices raising a child alone brings. As a child, you may have had a direct impact from these struggles. Over the years, it has taken some soul searching and deliverance on your part to forgive your father for turning his back on your mom and his unborn child. You envision what your life would have been like if both parents were present. You ponder if you could have had a "better life" or upbringing; but is this really the case? Afterall, your life up until now has molded you into the man you are today. Would you change who he has become?

You kept moving forward and did not let it slow your pace. Setting out to be the best gave you endurance to carry you through life's storms. You created bonds with others in lieu of having a broken relationship with your parents. You overcame tough obstacles, earned scholarships, finished high school and college, and became a business owner. You were the first person in your family to complete all these things. Yet still, you feel hollow.

Maybe your father feared raising a child, so he left, and that was his release. Maybe your mother had too many pressures of being a teenage mom, so she went out on the weekends and left you with your grandmother. That was her form of release. Maybe your parents yelled and cursed at you at the drop of a dime. This didn't have anything to do with you, but their distaste for one another was pinned up rage that was released upon you. Though these actions were selfish on their part, that was their form of coping. This directly impacted you and now you are questioning your worth. Despite all your accomplishments, you still feel like you aren't good enough.

Yes, your parents may have truly messed you up, but think of all those people who were there for you and who loved you unconditionally. The grandfather who taught you how to work on cars, the grandmother who embraced you with warmth, the aunts and uncles who supported you, the cousins who you laughed and joked with... those people poured love into your life. In retrospect, you were never alone, though you still felt lonely. Life is a place of second chances. To be truly happy you must release negative thoughts or feelings despite your past. Let the love of others help you to remove the pain and scorn that you harbor from your upbringing.

Now in adulthood, you seek to fill this loneliness. What about a partner? What about a wife? After all, you know how it feels to be abandoned and unloved, you would never do this to a significant other. But it's not the known hurts that people inflict on others, it is the unintentional ones. You need to be sure that you have completely healed from your past before joining to someone else.

In marriage, people always say, "You complete me," or "You are my better half." But contrary to these sayings, two half people should not join together. You both should first create full and wholesome lives for yourselves so that you can bring wholeness to your marriage. You try to encourage yourself to believe you can be a loyal, loving husband and you hope that you can find the same in a wife. You believe marriage is a concealed and divine joining before God that requires commitment like no other.

When you decide on marriage, you plan to spend all your life with that person. The good, the bad, and the ugly will all be exposed. Is it fair to her that you haven't dealt with the "me" before the "we?" A heart charred so badly must unite with someone capable of giving wholehearted acceptance, but that is a burden that you should not want to place on someone you love. First, you must protect your heart and heal so that you may be filled with love and compassion. You must bring your whole, fulfilled self to the table so that you won't unknowingly inflict your pains unto your future spouse.

You may have suffered during your childhood, but you are not damaged goods. Emotionally, your parents may have shattered you. However, your faith never trembled; God sustained you. The assumption would be that you would grow to be a womanizer. The brokenness in your life was alive and well. Many days and nights you prayed over your parents even though they wronged you. You realized that though you may have felt abandoned, you will not abandon them. The bitterness you held was that little boy crying out to be held; to be loved. But you cannot change your past. Instead, use it as fuel to launch you into the man that God called you to be. There are many others out there that are suffering from neglect and your healing and testimony can be their beacon of light.

CHAPTER TWO

Control His Thinking, Own His Actions

YOU CANNOT HIT BACK

"Humans are fearfully and wonderfully made." (Psalm 139:14) Our godly architect created us with such detailed precision that it's nearly impossible to duplicate our being. Science has been able to form skin for grafts, create an eye to replace vision, and construct prosthetics for those who may have lost limbs. But no one has been able to produce the one thing that makes us stand out among the other living creatures on this earth… feelings. Our emotions and the way we process and react to situations gives us a complexity that makes us truly unique. We can experience joys and pleasures one minute, and in the same day, be stricken with grief and heartache. Our feelings and emotions are our gift and our curse. By learning to control and understand these emotions, you can be the master architect of your emotional design.

American psychologist Paul Eckman pioneered the study of emotions and how they relate to facial expressions. With his studies, he found that not all expressions are a result of our culture, environment, and upbringing, but instead are biological, interwoven into our being since birth. These six basic emotions are fear, anger, joy, sadness, disgust, and surprise. Though you cannot change the emotions embedded in you, you can learn to control how you use and express those feelings.

At the most tender period of your life, you were taught to mask your pain. You would often hear "boys don't cry," when you outwardly expressed your hurt and frustrations which translated to tears. After a while, boys don't cry was embedded into your head and you learned to internalize your primal emotions. You were conditioned not to express hurt when you fell and scraped a knee. Instead, you were told to suck it up. When you were heartbroken by a first crush, you were told you were being too sensitive. Just the same, after a hard ballgame ending in a hurt arm or leg, you were told not to be weak. These reactions from the ones that impacted you the most scarred you. This petrified your emotions and compartmentalized your feelings. This was the norm, and the residue from your childhood deposited into manhood. You may think being able to "man up" is what made you a man, but this is furthest from the truth. This method of dealing with your feelings was learned but must be unlearned for the gem in you to truly be polished.

Adult events often trigger feelings of shame, fear, neglect, and abandonment, especially with significant others. While women openly express their feelings, you were conditioned not to do so. But now, your partner is requiring you to open up. She demands that you speak and voice your opinion. She requires you to be more loving. She longs for you to be more sensitive. She begs for you to be attentive to her needs. All the while, this is foreign to you because you've been conditioned to do the opposite all these years. You have these emotions, but it feels awkward to openly express them. This causes distress and tension in your relationships that lead to never ending arguments and disagreements.

The funny thing is, she lacks in areas of her own life as well. She may expect and demand certain requirements from a man, though she cannot do the same for herself. Opposite of you, she has been conditioned to be loving and caring. In return, she is told she should be taken care of and be the queen of someone's life. Though she has a career, she has been taught that the man is to provide. She has these life expectations because that's all she knows. This creates a tug-of-war of roles in which both need to let go of their end of the ropes and meet in the middle. This middle ground is communication. Neither of you can be each other's everything, nor should you be. Both need to be open and honest for the relationship to work.

Though she has her own emotions, she is needing you to bring those same emotions to the table. She wants to be able to lean on you for guidance and lend an ear when she is hurting. This is hard for you to do because no one has done this for you; you don't know how to do this in return. What she is requiring of you may not seem fair because you can't give something that you don't have. You are hurting, and as the saying goes, hurt people hurt people. You two are in a constant battle of trying to get each other to understand, when really, you don't understand yourselves. This leads you to feel that no matter what you do, she will never be satisfied. Afterall, what does she have to complain about? You provide for the household, you work hard, you go out on dates where you foot the bill, you bring her flowers, the physical intimacy couldn't be better, and you don't complain about her attitudes or mood swings. WHAT MORE DOES SHE WANT?! You have put your worth into question and feel attacked from every angle. But it's time to realize, it's not a *her* thing, it's a *people* thing. No matter how many material things you give her, no date night, flowers, or handbag can replace a truly genuine emotional connection. So even if you break up with her, you will have the same issues with the next. You must learn to unlock the most important elements in any relationship: emotions and communication.

> Change the changeable, accept the unchangeable, and remove yourself from the unacceptable." – *Denis Waitley*

It is important for us to recognize what a healthy relationship looks like. Not just with a partner, but with others. Sometimes, pain is confused with love while discomfort is associated with growth. For instance, you may have gotten used to verbal abuse, trash talk, or rude jokes from a boss or coach— *it just comes with the territory.* You may have an overbearing mother that meddles in your business and tries to control your life— *she just wants the best for me.* You have a girlfriend that hits you when she's extremely angered— *I was in the wrong. I'm a man. I can take it.*

This is not okay. This is not what caring looks like. For you to value yourself, you must recognize and voice mistreatment. You are not a punching bag. You are a man, and you have feelings. Voicing that your feelings and emotions are valid is the first step in recognizing this. YOU CAN HIT BACK. Once you own the true you, that will be the biggest fight you will ever win.

PERMISSION NOT GRANTED: MAN UP!

Coming to grips with reality is eating away at you. Your head should not be hanging low. All the requirements were met, or so you thought. For you, the responsibilities jumpstarted after you cut the umbilical cord, purchased formula, clothing, diapers, and new bassinet, started a second job and opened him a savings. Only to find yourself restless and immensely wounded.

All you wanted was to be better than your old man. Be the father that you always wanted. Give your child the things that you were not given. But your significant other makes this hard. The phone on the nightstand faced down, silenced calls, and ignored text messages soon led to late night creeps. You hoped your gut feeling wasn't true, but thoughts of her cheating are getting the best of you.

Your aspiration to be the textbook definition of a dad and to procure the fullness of a family now toys with your intellect. Idle mindedly, you strayed away from reality since you stayed away from the truth. Truth is, simple principles, faithfulness, and basic morals were deemed meaningless. Why did she devalue your importance after your child came? Naturally, the assumption would be her need from you had been fulfilled.

It feels like a horserace in your mind, faced with one question after another. Did she ever really want you or did she want what you could produce for her? Did she purposely dismiss you to see how much damage you could endure before the shattered break? Constant questions flooded your mind and her loyalty to you was questioned. Now, you have this tiny seed in the midst of drama. You are your father's child, but you don't want to father your child the way your father did. You dreamed of the loving household, but her constant nagging and excuses to leave has pushed you to a breaking point. You question her motives. You question yourself. You question the relationship. You question your sanity because you want to choke this woman for her blatant disrespect, but you cannot… hit… back. You entertain leaving, but you don't want your seed to grow up in a broken home. *What should you do?*

You entertain the idea of coparenting, but she will make it a living hell for you to see your child while milking you for child support. Her friends, family, and the rest of society will view you as a deadbeat when all you wanted was to have a stable home. The blame will be placed on you. Will your side of the story get an opportunity to be heard? You fear your absence will steer your son to ask the same questions that you asked many years ago to your father. "Daddy why do you not love me?" Heartache and despair will sink in, and no matter which way you turn, you will be penalized for your decision.

You have always heard that God counts the tears of the brokenhearted. Is being alone not equivalent to loneliness? You put your trust in her; it counted for nothing just walk away is what you told yourself. Life is composed of making hard decisions. As the journey continues, God fights the battle. Arriving to a place of peace and reinstating an adequate mindset of healing is essential. Maturation is happening for you, just hold tight and pull strength from all areas of your life.

> **Fear not, for I am with you; be not dismayed, for I am your God; I will strengthen you, I will help you, I will uphold you with my righteous right hand.** – *Isaiah 41:10*

Fatherhood isn't all it's cracked up to be, not because of the baby, but because of her. You feel confused, used, and unappreciated. Though permission from a woman is not required to be a man, you try to appease her. But how can you make someone happy that seems happier without you? You are beating yourself up over something that cannot be done. Until she finds her true self, she cannot be true to you.

The favor of the father is over you; he does handle your foes setting out to blight you accordingly. During one of your darkest moments, you were immersed in pain, you wept different now you move in silence. Everything in life comes down to choice. Making a conscious decision and putting yourself first will allow you to flourish. This may sound selfish, but you can't be self-less without learning what self is. To bestow proper love unto your seed, you must be in a place where you can provide proper water and nutrients. You cannot do this when the soil (environment) is toxic. Position yourself to where you are the best version of yourself, and then you can pour pure love into your seed. No more broken gems! It's time to protect your precious stone and break the cycle.

CHAPTER THREE

Unhinged

THE WORLD ON YOUR SHOULDERS ←

According to a study done by Cambridge University, the suicide rate for men is nearly four times higher than women. This is a staggering and unfortunate realization. This shocking difference among men and women leads us to ask one main question…*why*?

Traditionally, men are required to be the backbone of the household, the breadwinner, and the go-getter. No matter how much is on their shoulders, they are told to do better, go harder, and be stronger. Men are told to bottle up their emotions and not complain about tasks given. Heavy responsibilities are just something that comes with the territory. They are taught no matter how hot a situation may get, to walk through the fire and not fear getting burned. Any signs of weakness show that "you are not a real man," because after all, whatever doesn't kill you make you stronger. Right?

All these pressures dehumanize the man. At the core, humans, both men and women, have feelings and emotions. These emotions aren't meant to be concealed. Keeping them bottled up leads to a very robotic, shell of a man who bends under society's will. These bottled-up pressures make it seem impossible to be everything to everyone, which can lead to depression and hopelessness.

Voicing your emotions, struggles, and concerns is the first step to releasing this bottled-up stress. Sure, it's easier said than done, but it is like any other thing in life; it takes time to master. You need to work with yourself like you would work on a relationship or job. You cannot quit! You are worth it. You must relearn yourself over again. What makes you angry? What makes you tick? What makes you feel sad? What pushes you over the edge? Once you realize your triggers, then you can work on how to deal with those struggles.

The key is to tackle things one day at a time. If you look at the mountain, it will seem impossible to conquer, but if you only pay attention to your steps one foot at a time, next thing you know, you are climbing the mountain. It can be overwhelming when you try to handle all your emotions at once and it can come to the point where you just don't feel like doing it anymore. But when you take one day at a time, you will have the endurance to climb mountains and the faith to slay any giant that comes your way.

> **Therefore, do not worry about tomorrow, for tomorrow will worry about itself. Each day has enough trouble of its own.** – *Matthew 6:34*

Though counseling and therapy has become more mainstream in the recent years, it is still taboo among some ethnicities. For instance, in the black community you may hear, "What is talking to a stranger going to do for me?" Or "I'm not about to tell a stranger all of my business." This is a stigma that must stop. Just like the physical body, you must have check-ups and check-ins on the mind and spirit. If you have a broken leg, you wouldn't just wait it out and let it heal on its own. If you do, the pain can become unbearable, and in the process of healing, it can heal improperly. Just the same, for the mind and spirit to heal, sometimes you may need to enlist help. This doesn't make you crazy or weak, it makes you human. So, whether its scheduling time with a pastor or therapist, it is critical that you find proper healing to prevent extensive hurt and crooked healing.

Economic Confines

You feel that no matter what you do, you are unvalued in the workplace. Plagued from being overlooked, your dream job becomes a nightmare. Who wants to work and never get rewarded? You work hard in your position, many times going above and beyond. You arrive early and stay late. You eat lunch at your desk to meet deadlines. You do everything that is required of you, but still, you feel invisible. Something as small as a "thank you" will satisfy the hollow spot in your heart, yet these words are never uttered to you. So why even put in the effort?

Soon you start to slack, and work becomes mundane. You put in minimal input during meetings, and you count down the minutes until the end of the workday. Though your job may not be physically demanding, you are mentally exhausted. You thought that this would be it. All you ever wanted was a good paying job in the field that you earned your degree in. But somehow, this feels eerily similar to when you were working a warehouse job years prior. Initially, you were excited because you could work extra hours and receive time and a half. You would pack your lunch the night before and have your clothes prepared. After a while, this faded away. You started running in just in time to punch in. Your supervisor would get on you about your production quotas. You dreamed of the day when you had a profession where you were salaried and revered. Now that this day has come, it feels the same as the warehouse job.

Though the roles are different, the pressures are the same. No matter how you dress it up, you feel you just can't get a break. Is it your job to blame or is it your lack of motivation, inspiration,

> Do not pray for an easy life. Pray for the strength to endure a difficult one. – *Bruce Lee*

and enthusiasm to complete things when the going gets tough? No matter how high you climb the corporate ladder, you will always have demands. You must stop looking for rewards from others and start rewarding yourself. You are great at what you do, no matter if someone is looking over your shoulder or not. No matter if you are a student, a sanitation worker, an athlete, or corporate head, you must start working for *you*, not for recognition. Conquering goals start in the mind. Once you start setting goals for yourself, you will feel renewed in what you do. Recognition won't matter because you will genuinely enjoy what you are doing. Set forth small tasks daily, conquer them, and give yourself a pat on the back. You are your biggest supporter. It's time to get out of the slump and cheer yourself on.

At some point, the reversal must start. This stance in life is not moving. The expectation is to live. Your excuse is you are unsure what your next step should be. Your circumstances are your excuses. You are more than able to do better. Stop acting like you cannot clear those stumbling blocks. Fix your mind then you can face your problems. Get out of this phase. Stop sitting, waiting.

By gradually applying more effort, the shift from pity to phenomenal will feel natural. Don't let excuses stop you from crushing goals and being successful at what you do. You can be your own worst enemy and putting in partial effort only makes things more miserable. You thought if you had a better job, you would be happier. If you were paid more money you would put in the work. If you made your own hours, you would be more inclined to "show up and show out."

When you work hard for yourself regardless of the pay scale, reward, or praises, there will be a shift in the universe and something unexplainable will happen in your brain. You will be inspired, and you will stop making excuses. No matter what point you are at in your life, you will be motivated to go hard. It's time to make boss moves. Go back to school and get that GED or degree. Apply for that CEO position. Start that business. It's time to do this for *you*! Once you start stepping it up and being unapologetically you, outside influences and issues will become secondary and for once, you will propel yourself forward for *you*.

What economic constraints do you feel stunted your growth? Was it the neighborhood you grew up in? Do you feel limited to resources due to the color of your skin? No matter your situation, to experience true freedom, you must possess ownership. As the owner of your life and your situations, you decide what needs must be met, then you orchestrate a plan.
By staying dedicated to the process and working meticulously, you'll start to see God's manifestation birth life. Remember, though your achievements may prosper you financially, mental motivation will propel you into a successful, well-rounded life.

Who's to Blame?

Whether you grew up with both parents or raised by a single parent; whether you had a support system or had to rough it on your own; whether you grew up poor or well-off; or whether you were popular and talented or quiet and reserved— your view of finances is a direct reflection of someone or something. Did you have a father that gambled or a mother that frequented the casino? Did you have a parent that bought you the new Air Jordans every time they hit the shelf? Did you have a frugal upbringing where you were raised by a grandparent? These types of things shape the way we view and manage money.

Understanding the impact of your childhood will help you realize why no matter how much you obtain; you never feel fulfilled. How you view and handle finances shows your mental maturity. The more you get in your hands the more reckless you become. Money becomes expendable because you were never taught the value of a dollar.

You've convinced yourself that life consists of making money, paying bills, and repeating the cycle. Occasionally, you splurge or go on vacation, but you are constantly comparing yourself to others. All you think about is what you lack instead of what you have. Why are you focused on everything you are missing instead of the blessings right in front of you? This type of thinking causes fearful financial decision-making. You feel you might as well spend it now because what if you never get it again? Or that your income may not always be as much, so why not splurge while you can? This poverty mindset is leading you down a path of destruction.

When you have a poverty mindset, you fear that you will never have enough. So you overspend and buy things that proves your worth (expensive clothes, lavish items, foreign cars etc.). You value your worth and your status off of these "things." But things come and go. They perish and get old. They become "out of style" and no longer hold the worth that they used to. Therefore, spending your hard-earned money is merely a Catch 22, giving you a temporary high initially, but leaving you unfulfilled in the end. We must learn to discover true fulfillment and use money as a tool to achieve our goals. Easier said than done, but you must make conscious efforts and start taking small strides to change. Here's a few things you can do to break free from a poverty mindset.

1. **Learn to be grateful**

    When you are appreciative for what you have, you learn to count your blessings. When you are always looking for more, you tend to take for granted what you've already been blessed with. Remember, things could always be worse and even if they are not where you want them to be right now, there's still better days ahead.

    Don't judge each day by the harvest you reap, but by the seeds you plant. – *Robert Louis Stevenson*

2. **Start giving**

    Giving shows that you are concerned with the greater good. Even if your giving is minimal, contributing small acts of kindness makes the world a better place. Generosity shows that you wealth goes beyond yourself.

3. **Get out of your comfort zone**

    Start making moves. Shake up your current life. Change comes when you are outside of your comfort zone. When you hold on to things too tightly in fear of losing them, that's when you can't grasp on to anything else. When you move outside of your comfort zone, you'll start seeing spending, receiving, and giving in a new light.

4. **Adopt a new view on money**
   Read. Learn. Seek out new knowledge to expand your mind about wealth and capital. Learning will help to offset all prior inaccurate information about money. Also, try to delay immediate gratification. This will show you how much you have control over yourself, and your money.

   When prosperity comes, do not use all of it. – *Confucius*

5. **Pay attention to who you surround yourself with**
   Should you get new friends? Not necessarily. You are the average of the five people you usually hang around. Birds of a feather flock together. Look around you. You are becoming what your friends are. Rich people hang out with fellow rich people.

6. **Take responsibility**
   This one is big! Many times, we blame other people, jobs, and situations for our poor spending habits or not having enough funds to satisfy our wants. It's time you take responsibility. No one else is swiping that credit

card, buying those new clothes, or spending money eating out and/or partying. It's you. Learn to create a budget and live within your means. You are God's highest form of creation, use your intelligence to create the life you are meant to live. You must set limitations in order to position yourself for your abundance of blessings.

To be clear, we all find it difficult to deal with ourselves. Our voids are often driven by fear, accompanied with a huge lack of understanding. Breaking your habits involves changing your methods of operations. This will bring you resolutions for your mental battles. This shift will tremble you internally. Your life's compass will allow you to pinpoint those power struggles purging to the surface. By directing your focus to personal hopes, needs, and beliefs you will attract and gain clarity.

Undoubtably, you need to be persistent in staying away from the familiar. Feeling comfortable is a warning sign that you are not growing but being complacent. You must challenge yourself. By arriving to a place of recognition, you are able to take responsibilities for poor decision making. Holding yourself to a higher standard allows you to travel an avenue of learning. Recognize your blunders, learn from them, and continue with forward progress. Your yearning for a deeper understanding is the first step in allowing you to grow as a man. You will excel by making a conscious effort to remember your driving power.

Though finances and spending habits may have led you into pitfalls, it's never too late to gain financial knowledge. Your life is vivid, soon you'll be shining bright in lieu of worldly possessions. You are worth more than any gem, Italian suit, or foreign car. The gorgeousness of your value will be polished as you press forward. Do not waiver. Remember who you are, especially during times of uncertainty. Your faith will drive and steer you toward success beyond measure.

CHAPTER FOUR

Hard as Penitentiary Steel

How the Cards Were Dealt

In the previous chapters, we've explored factors that contributed to brokenness in men. By dissecting past traumas, current relationships, and societal issues, you were able to recognize the issues head-on and learn how to tackle them in order to provide healing, clarity, and wholeness.

The stories in this chapter will provide real life scenarios of men I know. These men entrusted me to tell their stories in hopes that they can help others find their way. While some stories may be difficult to digest, they are necessary to witness the healing process in full circle. As you read, you may find yourself relating to one or all of these men. We will explore their trials through the lens of their eyes and learn how they overcame them. Their stories will help instill hope in your current situation and provide encouragement for any battles that you are facing.

INCOMING CALL | RAYMOND'S STORY

We all expect a ringing phone to be answered, but this particular call I wish never penetrated my ear. I would have rather been annoyed by constant ringing, than to hear the piercing news that I received. No matter how many times I've replayed it in my head, I know that not answering wouldn't have changed a thing. I died that day, not physically, but I felt my heart was ripped from my chest while it was still beating. The world stood still, and all movement ceased to exist. I was frozen in time, and this was an incredibly heart wrenching moment to be in. I would never wish the pain that I'd experienced on anyone, but I know that I am not the only guy alive who felt the agony of being a dead man among the living. Who knew one call would make me feel like this? Who knew that one call would change my life forever?

Many presume that only women get postpartum depression. Contrarily, the arrival of a child was a scary change for both my wife and me. I was in my early thirties and had a great job. We readied our home to welcome the new addition. We checked off all the boxes. We were happy...we were prepared... so I thought. Soon, I recognized the level of stress parenthood carried was becoming unsafe and the aggressiveness grew to be frightening. RJ's life was dangling in the balance; an innocent soul that relied on his parents to love and care for him unconditionally. I tried, I really did, but it was the crying, sleepless nights, and the stress that kept us on edge. Those tense and disturbing events trigger moments of confusion. Thoughts of suicide and homicide dangled in the midst.

Depression resulting from childbirth for the father is viewed as taboo. The family dynamic was not what I dreamed it would be. Little RJ was in harm's way, and I didn't even realize it at the time. Now looking back, the eyes that should have been lovingly watching over him stared down in resentment. There was no doubt that we both loved him, but it was some sort of internal battle that we could not shake loose. I could tell my wife didn't want to be bothered with him. Where was her motherly instincts? But how could I judge her when I secretly was feeling the same? Feelings that overwhelmed my very being had me questioning my fathering abilities. I understood that I had to care and provide for him. My mind was congested, and it felt like I was going crazy. I leaned to her for help, but she would shoot me a look like, "How dare *you* complain?" Yes, it was true that she carried out the pains of childbirth, but I was carrying an unimaginable heaviness that I could not expel from my mind if I tried.

I was to a breaking point. I sought out counseling and attended alone since she refused to join. Why wouldn't she just accept the help?! Thoughts of her "snapping" plagued me while I was at work and when she was alone with the baby. I knew she was battling deep, depressive issues, but I hoped that one day she would eventually soften and grow past it. My therapy and treatment allowed me to understand my emotions and become stable and I prayed that my lead would help her adjust to motherhood while strengthening us as a family.

Soon, RJ flourished, and my faith grew stronger, but my wife still took a backseat in his life. As a young father, sleep should not be an issue. I was full of life, yet I still lacked energy. How does these two go hand-in-hand? I felt the need to sleep with one eye open. I was on edge; anxious. I'd turned over a new leaf and adjusted to our life, but what about my wife? I still felt a queasiness in my stomach, but I thought maybe I was just overthinking it. With all the therapy, maybe I evolved into a helicopter dad, always wanting to make sure my wife was tending to RJ properly. Daily, I assured her that she was not alone. We were in this together. We were a team! Still, I couldn't help to feel that she would rather sit the bench than put her full effort into the game.

Sunny days seemed grim. She would complain, cry, and become easily angered. She was convinced that he was possessed by some dark force and that's why his cries shrieked through the air in her presence. I assured her that this was not true, but no one could tell her otherwise. The curtains stayed closed to keep light out when I was not home. Her mind was convinced the sun made him respond to her in an ill manner. She started saying how much RJ hates her and how creepy his eyes were. The entire weekend, she was disgusted at the sight of her own baby boy. So, I would keep him. I would keep him as close to me as I kept my own heart. Sometimes I would be in and out of sleep for 72 hours straight. I was at a loss, and I was frustrated and irritated with her. Why couldn't she just snap out of it? How long was this phase going to last?

Then it happened. It was the call. One dreadful Monday morning, the phone begins to ring nonstop. I answered frantically.

"Hello?!"

On the other end my wife started to confess her ill intentions. She admitted that she'd been trying to drown RJ for the past week.

"Every other time he floated," she attested.

Unable to process what I'd just heard, swear words and name calling spewed from my mouth. I packed up as fast as possible, ensuring her that I would be home after lunch to get RJ and to take her to get the help she needed. I called her best friend to go sit with them until I got there, but her friend was unable to make it. I texted my mom to go by to do a safety check, but she refused to let my mom inside of our home. My mother frantically kicked at the wood slab, attempting to break in the door, but to no avail. My wife reassured her through the closed door that RJ was about to "go for a swim." My mom continued screaming and kicking as hard as her 87-year-old brittle limbs would allow her to, but it was in vain.

At approximately 11:32 am, I got another call. Hysterically, my wife screamed that the tub was full, and he was not floating. I pleaded with her to call for help and to get him out of the water, she refused. It was like something took over her as she responded with a dark, dehumanizing laugh.

My hands were tied. I reached out to the authorities explaining that my son was being drowned to death by his mother. I begged them to please hurry. I raced through traffic nearly killing myself to get there. That seemed to be the longest ride I had ever taken, even though I sped all the way home. Everything was moving in slow motion or standing still. I kept reminding myself that I should have done more. I was supposed to be RJ's protector. I noticed the signs. I blamed myself for not pressing her to get the necessary care.

Attacking myself only made the next phase worst. By the time I arrived, the police and emergency rescue vehicles were plentiful. The coroner pulled in directly behind me. *The coroner?* My wife was brought out in cuffs on her wrist and ankles. My eyes bounced around the scene. *Where is RJ?* An officer approaches me asking me to please provide a positive ID. *ID for whom? For my wife? For RJ?* My mind was scrambled. I couldn't grasp everything that was happening.

They took me over to RJ. His tiny, limp body was purple and black from head to toe. This was not my boy. This was not the RJ I remembered when I left the house earlier that day. The RJ I remembered gurgled while making teeny spit bubbles and smiled at me with his eyes. My heart wrenched. I fell to my knees in disbelief. The gravel on my knees felt soft compared to the hardness I felt in my heart. How could she do this to her own son? How could she take his life?

Her suppressed anger and delusions were way worse than I'd ever imagined. So now I'm left wondering… what if? What if I would have gotten her the help she needed? What if I was off work that day? What if her best friend was able to come over when I asked? What if the police would have gotten there a little bit sooner? What if my mother was able to breakdown that door? What if???

> **Our life is full of brokenness - broken relationships, broken promises, broken expectations. How can we live with that brokenness without becoming bitter and resentful except by returning again and again to God's faithful presence in our lives.** – *Henri Nouwen*

Fellas I won't lie, the pain never goes away. Any of you know, if you lose someone you love, you learn to move forward and persevere, but it doesn't mean "out of sight, out of mind." I will never forget my son. I will never forget the love that my wife and I once had. I will never forget the dreams that I had in the future for my family. But all of that was torn from me; ripped away like a bandage sitting on a scab. Honestly, I may not ever heal; I may always be broken. But you know what they say about brokenness… the worst kind of brokenness is the kind you don't know you have.

So, I stay prayed up. I learn to recognize and accept my brokenness. I stopped blaming myself for something beyond my control. I started ordering my steps in God's Word and not looking to my own understanding to figure out the "why?" The most important thing now is to figure out the "how?" How will I press on? How will I keep myself from falling into depression? How will I forgive my wife for something that is unforgiveable? There are four simple answers: prayer, therapy, forgiveness, and acceptance. God provided a way for you to deal with your broken heart, now it's time to take those strides to piece your life together again.

Captivity and Bondage | Daniel's Story

Raising children is hard. The saying, "It takes a village," is not an understatement. For children to grow and flourish into well-rounded individuals, proper care and guidance must be set in place. But what happens when it's not? What happens when the children witness acts of domestic violence among parents, hear the cries of the battered, sense the tension of the buildup leading to the abuse, and live among the aftermaths? These challenges are presented threats, putting children amid crises. Fear or flight mode come into play, but little hands know better than to fight back. For them, this is worse than captivity and bondage. They pray for the day that they break free but are imprisoned until they are old enough to come to the defense of themselves and others, or until they can flee their home.

I was a fleer. I ran away from my issues and rarely showed any anger or sadness. I was bottled up like soda, always shaken up and ready to explode, but my emotions found no escape and my lid stayed closed. Though I yearned for release, my aching voids were never filled. For this reason, I never knew true happiness. I managed to wear a façade most of my life to evade the pain buried deep inside. To most people, I was a great guy with a fulfilled life. Nice looking, decent job, humble… a pretty stable fella. However, they did not see how I often struggled with placing the appropriate emotions with the correct situation.

At 12-years-old, I was introduced to domestic violence at the hands of my father. Vehemently, he slapped blood from my mother's mouth. It flung to the ground like paint splatter, decorating our tan carpet with trickles of red. My father boldly justified his vile actions by saying, "That's what happens when the *king* is disrespected!" I will never forget the fear that trembled in my soul from that moment on. Now as a grown man, it still sends a cold chill up my spine when I reminisce on the treachery. As life progressed, I found myself dealing with my own crisis.

I met my ex-wife when we were young. She appeared to be everything that I wanted… cute, smart, and all about me. But it was the "all about me" part that made her psycho. Even before we were married, she acted like she owned me. It should have been a warning sign, but I swept it under the rug. For instance, she would cut her eyes in my direction if a woman spoke to me. Though it was innocent conversation, she couldn't stand it. She trembled with anger and would act out or curse me out when we got home. I should have recognized this as unhealthy behavior, but we loved each other, and I thought that a little jealousy just came with the territory. It wasn't long before it snowballed. Soon, I felt like a dog that was on a short leash, and every time she just pulled the chain harder and harder. It wasn't until after she had our first child that the monster grew, and the real craziness began.

One late night, I fell asleep with my baby girl in my arms while we were watching TV. I could feel it; I knew something was going to happen. You know that ill feeling that someone is watching over you while you are sleeping? Well, that's what I felt. Then it happened. This psychopath bit me on my face, down to the bone! She wouldn't release me. She was like a lion locked in on a gazelle. I laid there in excruciating pain holding my cheek with one hand and my daughter with the other. She said I was "resting too peacefully and not paying her any attention." I was in shock! Most people's initial actions would be to fight back, but all I could think of was my daughter witnessing that type of chaos. I didn't want her childhood memories to be the way mine was. So, I let it go. Little did I know, this was just the beginning.

I swore I would never tolerate domestic violence, but there I was. Why was this evil following me? It seems that children brought up in a hostile environment has a veil of darkness over their lives until their spirits are renewed. Ephesians 6:4 says, "Fathers, do not provoke your children to anger, but bring them up in discipline and instruction of the Lord." My father ruled with anger. He provoked everyone in the household and dared us to do something about it. He was a bully in which no one came to our rescue. Therefore, I felt the discipline and instruction of the Lord skipped over me and I didn't know where to turn. It was time for a renewing of the spirit but where would I start?

After being mauled in the face, I felt empty and worthless. I began questioning my manhood and feelings of loneliness were overwhelming me. I was not given any tools to cope with what had just happened. I had no idea how to leave her or escape this abuse. When the man is being abused, it seems that no one takes him seriously. I remember my uncle telling me not to be a chump. His explanation was that women are just crazy, and these types of things happen. Just don't provoke her and stay in my place. He left me with a "You'll be alright." But would I?

I ended up forgiving her and we moved in together. We were young and couldn't afford much, so we were approved for government housing. It was nothing fancy, but it was ours. This was the kind with bars on the windows and a deadbolt lock on the outside. It wasn't the ideal situation, but it was a place that we could call home, if you could call it that. This house ended up being my prison and no matter my escape plan, I was chained to this place.

She grew angry with me one day, like most days, but this day, she went to the extremes. She returned home with strangers bombarding our home, beating me without explanation. She heartlessly aided in the assault. I was left with two swollen, black eyes resembling a racoon, a busted lip, and a fractured jawbone. I was left curled up on the floor in fetal position and that's when she called her goons off like they were Pitbulls. Soon after, they left. Discombobulated, I couldn't muster up the strength to go to the hospital because I didn't know who she had waiting outside for me. So, I just laid there. She slept in the same bed with me as if nothing happened.

Tears soaked the pillow and I shivered wondering why me? The pain was too great to bear, not just the physical pain, but the pain in my heart. The night was long. I prayed for a glimpse of daylight… some sign to show me that a new day was dawning. I'd been reading the scriptures more and I remembered what was written in Isaiah 60:1-2, "Arise, shine, for your light has come, and the glory of the Lord rises upon you. See, darkness covers the earth and thick darkness is over the peoples, but the Lord rises upon you and his glory appears over you." As daylight peeped through the curtain, I had an epiphany. I locked her inside the house and went to the police station. I listened to the voice inside my head and snuck out when I had a chance.

I didn't realize until later that the same thing happened to three more her other children's fathers until I went to press charges. That's when the devil showed its face. She was on record and the other men also pressed charges at the same time. She was detained for approximately ten months. This was the hardest time of my life. Conflicted, I remembered wanting to drop the charges altogether, but law enforcement forewarned me that if I did, they could be brought up against me. Yet still, for the sake of our children, I pleaded for the minimal charges. The judge agreed to reduce her charge from criminal domestic violence to simple assault.

She had some type of hold over me. I couldn't pinpoint it or pry myself loose from it. We had a twisted love. I found myself working extra hours to save money, not for a smooth get away, but instead, to help bond her out of jail. Why free someone that was clearly a danger to me, my child, and apparently others? Sometimes, I thought I was just as sick as she was; I just couldn't shake this woman loose. Maybe I found some type of comfort in someone loving me so hard that they would do anything to keep me. My emotional stability was fragile, and she was a familiar space. She was home, in a sense. Because of this, I unyieldingly pursued freeing her. Then I did it. I freed her.

I re-enrolled in college which gave me the focus I needed. I found strength and began to be a better, more efficient constant provider for my child. I moved in with a family member and of course, she moved in as well. Shortly after, she became pregnant with our second child. I don't think she ever wanted him; I don't think she ever really wanted any of us, but her narcissist ways fed off control. I always tried to ensure our children how much they meant to us since their mother showed no real love or concern.

I tried my hardest to make it work to keep the family together, so I married her, but marriage didn't make things better. She disrespectfully bedded other men in our home. We ended up having five children altogether; three of which wasn't mine. She dared me to deny the kids and carried on with the mental and physical abuse. I was a stand-up guy. Those innocent babies had nothing to do with the sins of their mother, so I raised them as if they were my own.

After seven years of marriage, I was finally over it, and I conjured up the strength to leave her. Yes, we were tethered by our children, but I no longer wanted to be with her. I thought things would be easier, co-parenting from a distance, but the jealousy continued, and she made it hard for me to have a dating life. Questions flowed like a flood, accusing me of having other women around the kids. I told her that it was none of her business and that no matter what, our children were in good hands. She didn't like that. She despised me. She wanted to make me hurt. She wanted to make me pay.

It was a scorching summer day and she burned me for the last time. I took the kids to the fair and ran into my old high school sweetheart. We were excited to see each other, and it was great catching up and meeting each other's children. Then my ex-wife drove by while we were talking. What were the odds?! Later that night she came to my house and demanded I get in the car with her. I refused. I was done playing her games and I was no longer her pawn. That's the moment that all hell broke out. She jumped out of the car and pressed her way into the house. I was yelling for her to get out but didn't want to put my hands on her even after all she did to me. Our children also pleaded for her to leave, but she bulldozed through the house like a tornado. The kids cleared out of the way and stayed in the living room, knowing how crazy she could get. Then she gained the upper hand. She pushed me off balance near my bedroom, making me fall to the floor. Everything flashed before my eyes. Before I knew it, she savagely plunged a knife into my throat. Blood was everywhere. It was reminiscent of the blood that flung from my mother's mouth when my father backhanded her. I remember my mother doing nothing, but this was a moment I had to fight back, and I fought for my life.

    I gathered all the strength I had while blood spewed from my neck. There was a big nail sticking out of the was where a picture once hung. I flung her into it, and it pierced through the back side of her neck. I ran into her with all my strength, pushing her off the ground toward the ceiling. The nail ripped down the center of her spine and I cried out for my children. None of them came to their mother's aid, they were all on my side.

She ended up going to the hospital with no major injuries, and over time, I ended up healing as well. No charges were pressed on either end, but I just couldn't believe that she tried to kill me! I was with this woman from the age of 18 to 40 years old. A big part of me stayed for the kids, but in hindsight, it was more toxic for them to grow up in this type of environment than if we would've parted ways. I should have left long ago and raised the children myself, but I realize I can't go back in time, and I can't beat myself up over it. I couldn't let these children watch me crumble. I had to move forward. I had to persevere.

For years I had to walk on eggshells and let a lot of things slide. I believed in commitment, and I didn't believe in divorce. When I took my vows, I meant it. But at what point do you say enough is enough? I loved her despite the violence and infidelity. I loved her despite her crazy antics and flaws. I told myself that things would eventually get better, but they never did. I turned a blind eye to the men she had in *my* house, in *my* bed. I was lost trying to keep her happy, hoping that it would change our situation. I was so focused on her that I stopped paying attention to my children. My daughter started to rebel and display signs of loneliness, then my son began self-inflictions by cutting his wrist and thighs. This woke me up.

Broken Gems

I'm not going to lie, leaving was hard! I expected to bounce back after leaving her, but I was emotionally drained without the proper support channels. I expressed feelings of being isolated but discovered that solitude was important in listening to your own voice. Solitude helped to maintain my mental fortitude from the past, for the present and future. It helped me to find my worth and realize that I would never allow myself to endure this type of abuse again. I will admit, many times loneliness kicked in and stirred up emotions of pity and worthlessness. Was I so desperate for companionship that I accepted anything this woman threw my way? I accepted being bit, beat, stabbed, and cheated on. I accepted being treated worse than a dog.

Now that I'm out of it, I can see clearly. Sometimes, we need the veil lifted to know our true selves and our self-worth. The fact is, we were never meant to be, but I pursued the relationship regardless of the warning signs. Being unevenly yoked is worse than the venom of the saw-scaled viper. Now I know what I will and will not accept. Now I know what love is supposed to look like. Now I can forgive myself and love myself the way I should've all these years. Now I can be at peace and learn myself the way I should have many years ago. I know that God works in all areas of

> **The Lord is near to the broken-hearted and saves the crushed in spirit.** *Psalm 34:18*

our lives, even when we aren't working for ourselves. He is a heavy load lifter and a burden carrier, and I will continue to allow Him to comfort me. By trusting my intuition and putting things in God's hands, I know I will heal... fully and wholly.

Point Blank Range | Nikko's Story

I heard boots shuffling the ground. The crunch of the snow against the silence inside my house sounded like troops pounding the pavement. I was at war, but I was prepared. I knew they were coming, but where could I hide? My reign as kingpin had finally come to an end and I was ready to accept my judgement, but I refused to go out without a fight.

The thuds of the battering ram hitting the double doors echoed through the house. After several swift thrusts, the screws popped loose, and one door hit the ground like a ton of bricks. I immediately dropped to the floor and began a military crawl. I pressed my body hard against the marble floor, hoping it would swallow me up and I would disappear into it. Red beams shot through the house like lasers. Against the stark white walls, it resembled candy canes, but although it was Christmastime, I knew there would be no gift on the receiving end. I hadn't prayed in a long time, but in that moment, I raised from the floor, bent my knees, and hung my head. I thought it was over for good.

They knew me. They've been following me for a while and knew exactly how I moved. They were waiting for the exact moment to come in. Thank God my kids had just gone off to school and I was the only one home. I couldn't imagine seeing the terror in my little one's eyes. I would rather die than to see that. They found me in the laundry room, still in prayer position. I unclenched my hands, put them straight up in the air, then slowly clasped them behind my head.

"Easy... easy!" The SWAT yelled out.

I stayed in position, knowing that any sudden move could possibly end my life. They cuffed me, read my Miranda Rights, and presented me with a search warrant before ransacking my house. Though I didn't keep a lot of product where I laid my head, they did find a few bricks and a whole lot of cash. Soon, I was being shoved in back of a police car and carried off to the precinct. They had enough evidence and people who snitched on me to put me away for a long time. Soon, the US Marshalls were hauling me off to a centralized fed location.

My momma always said not to remove God from my life. But the more money I made, the more self-reliant I became. I became too big. I felt like I didn't need anyone, not even God. In a way, I became my own God. Years before, I used to be connected spiritually, but I felt in a way that God left me by the wayside. I grew impatient, not being able to make enough money, so I turned to the streets to get it the only way I knew how. Now that all of that was gone, what did I have? I had no one else to turn to, but God.

Now facing 40 years, the truth hit me. How did I get all these years when there are killers out there that walk free? But then again, maybe I am a killer. I was killing my community because of my greed. I'd surpassed making money to feed my family. I wanted the Ferrari and Benz. I wanted the big mansion... Scarface style. I didn't just want to be on top of the world, I wanted the whole world. And there I had it, it was in my hands, but all things must come to an end. I got careless because the life I was living became normal for me. Abruptly, my life slipped through my grasp and laid there like rubble. There was no way to put it back together. Just like that, it was over.

Thankfully, my kid's mom allowed them to visit me. Most women would be bitter when the money dried up, but I had a real one by my side. She was consistent. She put money on my books and made sure I wasn't in need. She took on the role of both mom and dad for those kids. She took on two jobs so that they didn't lack for anything. But as the years went by, I felt her slipping from my grasp as well. She was a good woman, so I knew it wouldn't be long before another man slid into her life. The news hit me like a ton of bricks. The letter that said she was leaving me came with no shock, but it still hurt like hell. It's like standing in the middle of the road and you see a bus heading your way. You know it is going to hit you; you know it was going to break every bone in your body. Just the same, I was crushed. I accepted it; I couldn't hold her back. That would've been selfish for me to do. I gave her my blessing and we still have unconditional love for one another till this day. She never wavered in being there for me when I needed, and she made sure I kept in contact with my children. For that alone, I will be forever grateful.

After a 20-year bid I was finally free. I was able to see my last two grandkids born and start building a relationship with my kids outside of phone calls and visiting rooms. I was free, but was I really? Unable to find a stable job due to my record, I started doing odds and ends. I ended up being the neighborhood handyman and I was good at it. One day, I got a call to fix a door. This young man's door got kicked in due to a drug bust. I knew he was headed down the wrong path and explained my story. He reminded me so much of me at that age, it seemed like I was looking in a mirror.

I gave him the lecture, but at that age, they barely listen. However, this young man was exceptionally witty, and he had an old soul. He didn't want to be part of the game, but that was all he knew. He said he wanted to start a construction company and with all the research of starting businesses and getting proper licenses and permits, I told him I could help. We crossed paths for a reason, we were there to propel each other into a better life.

Broken Gems

> I grew up in a community where I saw the process of how one becomes a drug dealer or a gang banger or a stick-up kid. There's a series of events that happen. People don't just wake up and decide they wanna be that. – *Michael K. Williams*

We had the skills. Soon, we were in business making the same amount that I was making before I got locked up. It was good to be legit and it felt good to buy luxury items. I was on top of the world again, but this time, without fear and without hurting others. Without seeing mothers sell their bodies for crack rocks. Without beating someone down who stole my "product." But most of all, I was proud I could save another young man from going down that crooked path. This is what life is all about. I now know that life is about decisions. No matter how much your back is against the wall, you always have a choice to do the right thing.

Struggle of the Captive Soul | Mont's Story

While my mother was a stay-at-home parent and my dad worked, I had outbursts that were unsettling. Mom and dad both were alcoholics; mom stayed in the hospital more than one could fathom and dad stayed in the streets. Dad badly beat my mom most days and I received a lot of whippings from him as well. The worst feeling was not knowing what I had done; sometimes he would wake me from my sleep with a belt in his hand and just started tearing me up. Education was low on the totem pole. As children, if my siblings and me didn't want to go to school, we didn't have to. Being the last child of ten, only two of my siblings finished high school.

With so many children in the home, it was difficult for my parents to effectively provide for all of us, so I had to make my own way. At age 11, my life started to take a horrible turn for the worst. I was not offered an adequate education to meet my learning challenges. I failed the 8th grade and the following year I had to repeat it. I displayed behavioral problems that were not controllable. I began fighting my peers, drinking, smoking marijuana, and being verbally aggressive toward others. The whipping that I placed on the principal was appalling.

I often struggled with reading comprehension, leaving me feeling dumb and out of place. I was not tested for an individual education plan to help me excel; all of the students were just lumped into one curriculum. The inner city during the 70s and 80s focused more on capital than education. Though I had compulsive disorders and learning disabilities, there was no real help within the public school system. Later in life, I was diagnosed with my disabilities. Maybe if I had help early on, I could have been more focused and driven to go in the right direction. But when you feel dumb, you feel helpless, and you find other things to fill that void.

I lived in a neighborhood that was not colored with positive features. The streets were drug, crime, and sex infested. It wasn't long before the career criminals and gang bangers introduced me to drugs and opened the door of crime to me. They pitched the script of fitting in and being a part of their family. I was expelled from school in the 8th grade for fighting a host of teachers, giving the choir teacher a heart attack. The smirk on my face would have made a normal person's skin crawl, but I didn't care. I was proud of the beating I put on them. These types of instances were the only accomplishments I knew; this was the only way I gained clout and recognition. In search of relief, at the age of 15, I began snorting cocaine and smoking an excessive amount of marijuana. Mad Dog 20/20 was my favorite beverage. My life soon took a cleft for the worst.

At this point, both parents began implementing and enforcing rules. My life was on a downward spiral. It seemed that drugs and crime were the only doors open to me. I was not only using drugs, but I started selling them. One can meet a lot of people living the street life and I happened to cross paths with Liz and Kelli (two sisters from Iowa). I started dating Liz. She and her sister, Kelli, was enticed by my attractiveness and laid-back demeanor. I was charismatic with a voice easy on words. I had a plan to change the game. I told them that I had a way that we could all make some money. Excited, the ladies were eager to not be broke again. I would bring guys to them, and they would charge them for arousal, stimulation, and erotic favors. Between the ages of 16 and 17, I felt I needed protection in the streets because of the amounts of money that was passing through my hands. I was initiated, affiliated, then protected. By the age of 17, I had nothing to worry about in the streets. I was the man, and with that, school and education never crossed my mind again.

Liz and Kelli were into a little bit of everything. We used to smoke marijuana together, but I knew they would do more than that when I wasn't present. One day I was tense and weed just wasn't doing it for me. That's when they presented it to me. The two sisters offered me to smoke crack cocaine with them. Though they were prostitutes, they didn't appear to be like the cracked-out people I'd encountered, so I thought why not. I did it. I hit it and it took me on a high I didn't know was possible. Till this day I wish they hadn't presented it to me. To this day I wish I'd never met them. I'm not playing the victim, but I do feel that if I hadn't associated myself with these two, things may have been different.

Soon, I was getting high on my own supply. I thought I was in control of the crack honestly. Who in the world sets out to be a crackhead? I surely didn't think I would. I thought I was stronger than that. A little recreational drug wouldn't hurt to help me escape reality. I figured that since I kept myself up, no one would know the difference. I dressed nice and remained well groomed. The truth is, I had no idea how to control the monster inside. I shifted from selling crack to smoking crack. I started lying, stealing, and begging to get it. Anything to get "a hit."

I knew a lot of people, including a lot of women. Lyric was one of them and was a "free spirit" to say the least. Several guys I knew from the block had taken turns flipping the pages with Lyric. She had a lot in common with the 24-hour corner store— Always Open. One day someone called the cops on us while we were all at my homeboy's house. Out of nowhere, the police pulled up then took all of us to jail. I went to prison for the first time at the age of 16. I was falsely accused of sexual assault, distributing a control substance to minors, sell of a controlled substance > 50g, and sex trafficking. The statement "being in the wrong place at the wrong time" perfectly described my situation. Sure, I was guilty of selling drugs, but I never laid a finger on that girl. I was no rapist or sex predator. Never touching Lyric has haunted me until this very day. None of my DNA was found on her, in her, or on the scene.

While fighting this case and awaiting my trial date, I was arrested again for selling heroin and stealing my attorney secretary's pager. My cousin was dating her and asked me to take it so that I could get the numbers out to see is she was messing around with anyone else. I was losing hope. Seemed like every corner I took was a bad turn. Due to my drug use expenses, I had exhausted all my money. I was dried up, so my paid attorney dropped me. At this point the state picked it up and issued me two appointed lawyers. I was shattered. It seemed that no one wanted to fight for me. I was just another face on a case. Within a month of attaining the appointed lawyers, I was given a chosen jury selected by not one, but two inexperienced lawyers. Found guilty without any evidence or witnesses gifted a 20-year sentence.

In the process of all these life changing circumstances, my girlfriend tells me that she's pregnant. She gave birth while I was incarcerated, and I feared never being able to see my baby girl. Regrettably, her mother moved her far away during my imprisonment. Father and daughter did not have the opportunity to have a wholesome relationship from conception. The theory was that we both have made significant efforts to at least love one another. Lies, walls, and time snatched my baby girl from my reach.

During my prison stay, experiences happened. Including every type of abuse conceivable. The details are too sad for discussion, so lets' leave it at that. I'm just blessed to have survived in there for 15 years. Finally free, I was no longer in captivity. But my freedom didn't remove the remnants of the excruciatingly painful years. I was placed on highly addictive pain medication and given meds for stress and depression. I was prescribed psychotropics to keep the voices in my head and suicidal and vicious thoughts at bay.

My family and I talked it over and decided it was time for a change in scenery. I relocated to a tranquil, low crime neighborhood. Life was much easier; gun violence, prostitution, and drug crime were rare. With drugs far from my reach, boredom ignited my crack smoking addiction again. I started back smoking crack cocaine and marijuana, and when my family found out, they detached themselves from me. My disinclination to change had driven a wedge without recoil between the family. Once again, I gave crack credit...it was in control. I felt it helped ease the constant battle of thoughts from my past. In particular, the wrongful convictions case and all the turmoil that followed. I didn't have to think about my sins and emptiness. I didn't have to deal with reality.

I feared people's perception of me since I was now a registered sex offender. I knew I didn't do it, but the truth didn't matter to them. Sadly, my extensive record and life of crime didn't help. I was to blame. Even though wrongly accused of rape, I set myself to be a target for the judicial system. I was cutting corners on the street of denial, but I didn't know how to find genuine help.

I often felt attacked by life, people, the system, and drugs. I was up against an unworldly attack. I felt as if I was losing a battle and failed to find refuge in the darkest places. I thought that viewing life through a different lens might erase the long trail of defeat. Instead, I opened doors to lying, stealing, money, women, drugs, and my past. I knew I had to get out of the drug use comfort zone.

Ironically, I continued with my lies, even after relocating again. I decided to try to start over with my new girlfriend after the death of my father. The local poultry plant hired me, so I was finally making honest money. Ecstatic about life, I was able to provide for my future wife. She was amazed by my drastic life change, and I was happy that I was finally able to make someone proud of me. Some time went by, and I thought I had it all together.

Regrettably, drugs were still present and a huge part of my life. The drug use got worse, and control was not in sight.

One day, I lied to my girlfriend about where I was going in order to get a fix. In the hotness of summer, my skin was sticky, and my veins were pulsating. I needed drugs. As I approached the drug dealers house, I noticed an assemblage of law enforcement present. Before I could make the block and get away from there, I was pulled over and arrested. My charges were driving without a license, drug paraphernalia, and two murders. *Another wrongful conviction*, I thought, but God showed me His mercy and grace. After being incarcerated for a few months, all charges were dropped against me. This was my opportunity to take a different path.

After relocating from state to state, change was something I was familiar with. But no change of scenery would fight off the demons that was tagging along. No matter where I went or how I got there, they were along for the ride. Despite this, I reassured my girlfriend that moving to another state would be a good thing and a fresh start. And it was… initially. Just like all fresh things, they become stale after a while and the molding process begins.

Upon moving to the new city, I met a guy named Red who paid me $3 to $4 per car to help detail vehicles. Though that was merely pennies to me, it was an honest living. But money was coming too slowly, bills were piling up, and my patience was running thin. I realized then that suffering and patience often goes hand in hand; and I needed to be strong enough to endure both. If I was just a little more patient, waited a little bit longer, and worked a little bit harder, I would have saw new opportunities on the horizon. I wasn't thinking clearly and strategically. After hastily evaluating the situation, I became overwhelmed, and life became dark again. It felt like every open door kept shutting on me, leaving me standing on the outside alone. There's only so long that you'll stand knocking at a door before walking away. I felt only a fool would stay, sitting on the front porch, waiting for someone to come home. I knock a few times and when I get no answer, I leave. Just the same, I couldn't wait any longer, and sought out other sources for comfort.

Drugs and stealing had overtaken me, and I didn't have the tools to endure. I began criminally trespassing at every store in the city, which was a total mortification to my girlfriend. So, she left. She left me in the city to fend for myself and moved away without me. I never seen that day coming. I pleaded to go with her, but she told me that the only place I needed to go was rehab. Even though I begged her not to leave, she stood her ground. This was confirmation for me, and I knew I needed rehabilitation. I was down on my luck and ready to give up on life. I tried taking small steps in the right direction, but it's not that easy to become freed from drug addiction and crime.

    After almost killing myself on a three-day drug binge, I checked into a drug rehabilitation center. I stayed there a few days then left. The law was waiting on the other side, and I was sentenced to 1 ½ years in prison for my petty crimes. After my time was up, I tried rekindling things with my girlfriend. She told me that I couldn't come to live with her, but I went anyway. When I got there, she had a male roommate staying with her. She never told me this because she didn't want to hurt me, and she also didn't want to deal with my mess. In the dead of winter, I was homeless, sleeping in a car, and surviving once again the only way I knew how. I engaged in a sexual relationship with a known prostitute that offered me "Ice" otherwise known as Crystal Meth. By this point I was feening. I wanted to feel something, and I also wanted to feel nothing. I took it. I indulged in it. I loved it. I didn't think of the repercussions of these actions, but I could truly say, that was the last thing on my mind. I didn't think, that was the problem. I didn't care, that was the other problem. I didn't realize how much my actions affected those who loved me. When my ex-girlfriend found out I was using Meth, all emotion drained from her face. It was a blankness, not a cold stare, but a sad one. I knew that I hurt her beyond measure, but I didn't know how to fix it; I didn't know how to stop.

I've tried reading bible scriptures and passages. I've tried going to church. I've tried staying away from drugs. But I guess I wanted the "feeling" more than I wanted to help myself. I felt like a fisherman lost at sea and that Siren kept calling me...singing to me... luring me back to her. People smoke cigarettes every day and know the risk of cancer. People drink alcohol all the time and know the risks of liver disease. People have unprotected sex, and know they have the risk of catching an STD. How am I any different? These are those people's drugs of choice. Just because they aren't shooting up, snorting up, or smoking up street drugs, doesn't mean it isn't a vile addiction. They have their drug of choice, and I have mine.

One day with God's help, maybe I can recognize my triggers and learn how to avoid these behaviors. I know that I make hasty decisions and caused self-inflicting pain during times of uncertainty. That's when I go back to the familiar; that's when I go back to the thing that comforts me the most. Until I figure it out, I'll nestle in her bosom like a baby and let her hold me tight. Hopefully she won't smother me. Hopefully, one day I'll leave her arms.

FOUND IN THE GRAVE | TRE'S STORY

The faster obstacles came, the harder I fought. I've dominated some of the toughest street battles, soundlessly escaped homelessness, and broken generational curses. Mentally and physically, I have been through hell and back. But out of everything in life I've been through and out of everything that I've overcame, nothing prepared me for this next hurdle. Blindsided, I did not see this coming.

Eleven months ago, I started experiencing seizures and blackouts. The day was dreary and dim, accurately reflecting how I felt inside. Doctors informed me that my life may never be normal again due to the syncopates and seizures. The medically educated could not figure out why the seizures or syncopates were happening. After extensive testing, they decided it was best to put me on medication. Never had daily prescription medicines been precedence in my life. This was a first for me; I was terrified!

I had two choices: either give up life by feeling sorry for myself or persevere. It was a simple decision. I understood that we are all created and provided with the gift of choice. My mind was made up and I knew deep down that God had a plan. His plan, no matter how dim things looked, included my health and survival.

For as long as I could remember, leaving a legacy filled with value and impact is what pushed me to thrive. It starts with relationships. I was ready to fight and continue to be the rock and provider for my wife and children. I had a traveling job that I loved, but when I informed my employer about my seizures and syncopates, my position was reduced to a desk-ridden paper pusher. My mind was playing tricks on me. My mind was telling me that my manhood was reduced by my job status. But I had to combat the negative mindset and realize that I was still working and providing for my family. I recognized that it's not the job that makes the man, but the man that makes the job. I knew that it would be alright. It was time to embrace change. I knew that I must be empowered to move toward the idea of change. By taking the first steps, God's glory would entrench me with love and resilience. I was geared up to fight this thing and I was going to win. I was determined, and with God's blessings upon me, I knew that things would be okay. Change had always been difficult for me, but I knew it was time to face that giant.

  It wasn't easy, and it still isn't. At 40 years of age, my family dynamic went from normal to complex. It was like learning to function with dysfunction. The children were somewhat afraid of what could happen at any moment.

> **Don't give in to stigma. A diagnosis does not determine who you are or what you can do!**
> –Van Rankin.

As you can imagine, it's difficult to console young minds or even help them to understand. They want to help, and they don't want to see their parent suffer, but there is nothing they can do. At times, it makes them feel helpless; it makes me feel hopeless.

But this is something that I must live through the rest of my life. Medicine keeps it at bay mostly, but it is optimism that keeps me going. Of course, I am saddened at times, but I must always remember... I... AM... A... CONQUERER! Each day I fight a new battle. Each day I *choose* to live. Some may view my seizures as a setback, but I view it as a set-up. A set-up to live on purpose and with purpose. A set-up to treat each day as a gift instead of taking it for granted.

Many people feel as if when they are diagnosed with an illness or condition that it is a death sentence. Well, I'm here to tell you that you are not dead... you are very much alive! You are not yet in the grave, so make your days on this earth count! Even the healthiest person can be living their best life and have their life snatched from them in a blink of an eye. So, cherish life. Appreciate your circumstance. No matter how bad it seems, it can be worse and no matter how tough things can get, it can always get better.

> **Although the world is full of suffering, it is also full of the overcoming of it.** – *Helen Keller*

I am here to give my testimony. I am an overcomer because each day, I purposely live another day. I'm not going to lie, it was tough at first, but this is my reality, and everyone has their own burdens. At the end of the day, it's all about your mindset. We allow ourselves and others to pour into us daily. Do you view your life as half-full or half-empty? Once you learn to control your mindset, you can change everything. If I can lend one bit of advice it will be this, no matter your situation big or small, you can move forward... you can live... you can persevere!

CHAPTER FIVE

Solitaire Confinement of the Mind

PREPARE FOR THE FLOOD ←────────

After reading the young men's stories in Chapter Four, we realize that trials and tribulations are inevitable. Consider that it's not *what* happens, *when* it happens, *where* it happens, or *why* it happens; it's *how* you handle these tough times that matters. But how do you prepare for the flood? Let's take the story of Noah's Ark. He was instructed to prepare for the flood by building an ark large enough for his family and two of each species of animal on this earth. This seemed ridiculous to so many people and there were lots of naysayers. It seemed unnecessary to build this huge ship for a storm that may never come. However, it did come, and he was prepared. When this flood came, none of the naysayers could save him or his family, he saved himself by preparation. We must do the same with our minds. No matter how many people you have around you, they cannot save you from yourself or your situation. You can only do that.

Preparation of the mind and spirit is necessary to be able to handle the weight of life. For instance, if you've never bench pressed, would you start off with 250 pounds? First thing is that you wouldn't be able to lift it. No matter how much you strained and grunted, it just wouldn't happen. If you were able to lift it, you would surely risk injury. Your body is not prepared to handle that much weight that quickly. You must start slowly. Lift the bar first. Over time, add more and more weight. Challenge yourself. When the time comes, you will have built enough muscle that you will be able to lift heavy and reduce your risk of injury. Just the same, you need to train your mind. Don't try to start this training all at once but start with small exercises. This could be short meditations, prayer, reading self-help books or seeking out counseling. Each thing will grow your mental muscle to help you not break under pressure, but instead, prepare you to carry the load.

Do you sometimes wonder why does it feel as if your wheels are always spinning? You are stuck in a rut, still in the same spot. Even after all the advice and lecturing, you still can't get going. It's like you know what to do, but you can't get started. The clouds of doubt are suffocating you and it feels like you are going down. Don't crash! There are many resources to help you if you just make the first step. Sure, it may feel awkward at first, but the more you work on your mindset, the more natural things will feel. You'll find yourself getting less angry and learning to manage your stress efficiently.

There will be times that you feel overwhelmed, scared and alone. These times *will* come. Sometimes there will be flood after flood and the storm just won't seem to go away. It comes through like a wreckage, leaving behind limbs and debris. You are left to clean up the mess; you are left to pick up the pieces. But how can you do this when every piece of you is broken? How can you mend?

These are the times you need to take refuge. You may feel that doing the right thing is getting you nowhere and no breaks are coming your way. As grim as this may sound, thoughts of peace often appear in a dark pit of pain and worthlessness. Sometimes it is those quiet moments after the storm that you can see things more clearly. The clouds will roll away and the sun will shine again. There will be a little still voice guiding you. Some call it intuition, some call it God, and some call it a guiding light. No matter what you call it, it is there. It is always there. You just have to quiet the outside noise to be able to listen and accept guidance. Let the evolution of understanding take place.

Migrating through feelings of fear, rage and hate, forgiveness, and weakness is creating a storm inside of you. You may be afraid of what people might say if they know you are seeing a counselor, seeking therapy, or taking medication. You fear they may laugh, downgrade you or think you are crazy. But the definition of being crazy is to be foolish, unwise, senseless, and deranged. But isn't it foolish and unwise to not seek help? Is it not deranged to keep acting out of anger in hopes to remedy your situation? There will always be people who says nasty things because they are unsure of themselves. They don't know how to handle their own situations. They don't know how to prepare for their floods. Therefore, you are not the crazy one, you are the wise one who recognizes your needs and caters to your wellbeing.

Once you learn to direct your attention to areas of self-contentment and meditation, darkness will no longer plague your life. Through the discovery of happiness and self-value, the black hole in your life will dissipate. These are the aspects that allow you to navigate through chaotic lines of turmoil from a place of unrest to a place of delight with that sweetly, softened taste of relief.

Why?

"Why" is the interrogative adverb that will take you into a tunnel where you may feel that you cannot move forward. You may feel stuck, claustrophobic, and your breath may become shallow. Indeed, life can subjectively be compared to a blank state of uncertainty. The mundane, absent thoughts of possibilities for success in a society designed to demolish you can seem surreal at times. This can create a wind tunnel where you find yourself fighting to stand.

Your mind can be like an ambiguous tunnel if you don't know how to navigate through it. Lost in your own thoughts, the channel gets longer and darker. It seems unending. Inside the tunnel, you hear the question, "Why have you done nothing to change your circumstances?" For most of your life, you've allowed fear to be the excuse…fear of failure… fear of rejection.

> **Believing and investing in yourself is the best way to shift your thinking from a paradigm of excuses to one of solutions.** – *Farshad Asl*

As a safe haven, you find solace in the tunnel, even though it's cold, dark, empty, and lonely there. The path may be long and composed of a rugged terrain, but if you keep pressing forward, you will see light at the end of the tunnel. Your emptiness is overwhelming, but you can't allow loneliness to triumph the persisting emotion tapered beneath the surface.

At times, you feel detached from everyone and want to be by yourself. That has been the driving force for the sensation of your loneliness. Some days, things may just kick off the wrong way and no matter the effort. Even those close to you can't put vice grips on your pain. This can make you feel like an outcast. You're diligently committed to prayer, but in your mind, you don't feel like it's working. You know that God always comes to your rescue…but you can't help but feel the Lord's distance. You feel abandoned.

In the tunnel, discoveries about your animal circles are coming to the forefront. No pause, no commercial breaks, no explanation, and no chance of understanding. With your faith in God wavering, you start putting your trust in man. You feel that if you create friends and bonds, they will never let you down. This is the way BJ felt.

Broken Gems

BJ was a young man who had good grades and was very family oriented. He would help his elderly grandmother do her grocery shopping and assist his mom with bills when he could. His mom worked double shifts at her cleaning job and would often come home with aching bones and throbbing feet. But even though she worked ceaselessly to provide for the household, it still wasn't enough. Many times, there was only cereal for dinner, in which the milk needed to be watered down to make it stretch. Although she was barely able to provide, she didn't qualify for Food Stamps. It was a Catch 22. Either sit at home and rely on the government or work and hope you make ends meet. BJ's mom was humble and didn't want to be part of the system, so she chose the latter.

> **It is better to trust in the LORD than to put confidence in man.** – Psalms 118:8
>
> **Don't trust anyone, not your best friend** – Micah 7:5-6

BJ would often look at his two younger siblings. Though they smiled, he saw the pain in their eyes. Not having enough food to eat was minimal to the fact that they were suffering from not having their momma around. He knew he had to do something. But what? Since he was an introvert, he had no friends to turn to, so he broke out of his comfort zone and found ways to establish friendships. He knew that there were kids from his neighborhood, just like him, that knew ways to get money, legit or not.

In time, he proved himself as being loyal by doing small tasks given. Soon, he ran with a crew, and they all had each other's backs, so he thought. Just because he was solid, didn't mean they were. Everyone that cross our paths aren't on the up and up and some may have similarities to those that embrace hell's fire and brimstone. It's our choice to decipher how to decide whom should stay or who should go. Unfortunately, BJ chose the wrong group to stay.

One day, his squad conspired to rob a group of convenience stores on different sides of town. They had an inside connection at each location, so they figured it would be a quick hit and an easy come up. Each store had a safe that held several thousand dollars. Though they wouldn't be rich once it was split, it would be enough to help BJ pay up his mom's bills for a few months until he landed a job.

"In and out," they told him. "All you have to do is drive."
So, he did.

His partners masked up and ran into the stores. One… two… three stores down. In between time, they hid the money in various spots for safe keeping. There was already more money than they had anticipated, but greed set in, and they kept the original plan to move on to the final location. BJ had an ill feeling in the pit of his stomach, but he was too deep in now. They all jumped in the car to head to the last convenience store.

BJ didn't need the flashy shoes or named brand clothes. He just wanted enough to help his momma. But on the way to the fourth store, sirens swarmed around them like bees during pollination. Red and blue lights were everywhere.

> "Just be cool man… just be cool." One of his buddies tried calming an anxious BJ. His clammy hands gripped the wheel so tightly that his knuckles began to hurt.
>
> "We all got records besides you. They'll let you off easy, but if we take the wrap, that's it for us." another said, voice trembling.

No more talking. At that moment, all four boys were commanded to exit the vehicle with their hands up.

> "You thought you were gon' git away with it, didn't cha?"
> One cop barked out before spitting on the ground.
> "We got cha now!"

When asked whose vehicle it was, BJ dedicated his loyalty to his crew and said it was his, even though it was stolen. Inside the vehicle was guns and weed. They took the boys back to the precinct and questioned them individually. Somehow, everything got pinned on BJ.

Blinded by everything that his homeboys promised, he had no idea what was up ahead. On a warpath of amplified emotion, he was convicted while the other three culprits roamed free. The judge made an example out of him and contrary to what he thought would happen, he received a long sentence.

> "Maybe the next time you will choose your friends more wisely; those three they conspired against you."
> The judge uttered in a monotone voice.

His homeboys were free to take trips out of state while BJ took a bus trip upstate. Uncanny, the question remains unanswered, *why?* Why would his friends desert him after he sacrificed himself for them? The people he thought had his back turned their backs on him. Now, he retreated to his tunnel hoping to find comfort, but the darkness he finds there just makes him feel oppressed and alone.

BJ put aside everything for friendship... his values... his dignity... and his faith. Now who was left to turn to? He'd ignored counsel from his loved ones who told him to stop hanging around those boys. They only wanted the best for him, but he didn't take heed to their warnings. He thought that they were in his business, or just trying to tell him what to do. But they really did have his best interest at heart, and if he would have slowed down to listen, just a little, then maybe he wouldn't have been led astray.

> Like a muddied spring or a polluted fountain is a righteous man who gives way before the wicked. – *Proverbs 25:26*

As his life continued to be intertwined in shambles, perplexity revealed power in opposition. Bewildered, thoughts of worthlessness flooded his mind. How could he help his mom and siblings from behind bars? The poverty-stricken situation aided the process as well. His emotions were behaving in a state of misperception. He was a child taking on an adult role to provide. He had no real plan to rectify the situation.

After spending a couple of years in a cell, BJ heard voices in the tunnel instructing him to give up, stand down, and die. He felt he had nothing to live for. Twelve years for a 17-year-old seemed harsh; he knew that he wouldn't embrace freedom until he was nearly 30. Drowning in wonder, he kept replaying the day over and over in his head. He later learned that his homeboys got off by snitching on a bigger fish that the Feds were looking to fry. The three took the rest of the money and walked away scot-free without any repercussions. They didn't even have the decency to help BJ's mom as she faced eviction from their duplex.

BJ was serving his 12th and final year of prison when he got the news that his mom passed away of a heart attack. All that he did 12 years ago was for her to have an easier life, but all he did was make her life harder. His sentence was served in vain. She continued to work hard until the day she died. Under high stress, she struggled to send him money for basic necessities during his stint. Reality is, no number of socks, underwear, or white tees will ever bring her back. One bad decision on one day led BJ down the tunnel of destruction. What if he didn't participate in the robberies? What if he wasn't the driver? What if he didn't take the rap for everyone? What if he waited to find a legit way to make money? What would you have done in BJ's shoes? What could he have done differently?

The flip Flop

The dark side leads to periods of pain and turmoil. Regardless of your emotional awareness, you may find yourself, *pondering where did I go wrong?* There will be times of great uncertainty and grey areas. On those desperate days, strongholds are in full affect.

Face-to-face with emotional and mental discomfort, dependency, isolation, misinformation, control and self- worth issues, anxiety, fear, suicidal and homicidal ideations, seduction, and past abuse, instead of flipping your mindset, you are expected to flop. Superficially and wretchedly, this emotional turmoil ignites with sparking a flame on the mind.

From reading BJ's story, we realize that it's sometimes who we surround ourselves with that can bring out the worst parts of us. Staying loyal to friends and family who uses you for personal gain creates toxic relationships and can lead you down the road of destruction. It's time to cut yourself lose from these types of people. Yes, it may feel lonely at first, but these people are like quicksand, pulling you down slowly. It's time to show loyalty to yourself and your mental and physical well-being. Keeping these relationships will only bring pain. It's like turning the stovetop burner on high, then reaching for the flame. Why touch it if you know you are going to get burned? Just the same, why keep lending your energy to those who you know will end up burning you in the end? It's time to turn that burner off so that you don't get scorched by the flames.

When you decide to change it up and flip to the other side, it can be confusing. Some of these people have shown you love at your lowest points... how can you cut them off? It's difficult to distance yourself because you remember the good times and how they made you feel when they are around. But life is more than feeling, it's about healing. Some of these people have taken advantage of you or abused you physically or mentally. Distancing yourself will allow you to not succumb to this treatment anymore. Sometimes when you are in it, you don't notice the detriment it is causing to your life. To break free from the bondage, you must recognize that this is a problem. The cycle of narcissistic abuse will go on until you find the strength and power to put an end to it. It is only you. No one else can stop it for you. Education on self-absorption is important to learn. Do not let them pour poison into your sponge. How does the narcissist brain work? Emotional control, remorse, the absence of compassion or empathy are ever present.

You may feel the wheel turning and entertain the idea of change, but change is often difficult. You know that You are better off without these people in your life, but you fear loneliness, ridicule, and isolation. Talking to a therapist can help you work through these emotions. Not only is a therapist trained to deal with issues just like yours, but they are an outside resource that has nothing to gain. Unlike those that surround you, they are around you for a reason. Whether that is for emotional, financial, or selfish gain, your best interest isn't at heart. With a therapist, they want to see you heal from your situation; they want you to succeed. They can help you decipher the real from the fake and they can help you learn how to comfort yourself instead of relying on those that can hurt you. It's time to take the next step. Like a coin, you can flip and land heads up. You can win!

Strength, acceptance, patience, and a strong mindset can give power and mental stability. Gaining control over your emotions help bolster you mentally. Resilience makes you more functional and successful in society. Anyone can become better at regulating their emotions. Proper structures are indispensable. It takes practice and dedication just like any other skill. Suppressing your emotions does not help in any kind of way. Flip before you flop into another spot of uncertainty.

Therapy isn't your only option to start your self-discovery journey. You can start today by acknowledging your feelings. Start speaking up and being transparent with people mistreating you. Recognize that negativity of the mind has no hold and you; you are in control. Learn to change your outlook on things even if they seem negative. Know that if you wake up on the wrong side of the bed, you did not awaken on the floor. You can turn the day around by controlling your emotions. Calm yourself, breathe, and direct your attention to the positive. By taking a different approach it can help you relax your mind instead of becoming irritated and angered.

The best way to get a different perspective about the next step of a problem is not to make speculations. Focus on the facts. You do not have to wonder why. If you find yourself dwelling on something negative, find something that will clear your mind. In the beginning this will take work, but over time, you will adopt this as a natural thought process. At first you were fragile, ready to break at any moment and crack under pressure. Below the surface, you felt constrained from freedom and had a life plagued with treachery that weighed you down mentally and physically. Once you take a leap of faith and learn to trust yourself, the pressure will be lifted, and you will be renewed.

The Educator's Guidance

Family and educators are the first groups that shape our personality, attitude, morals, and values. If you grew up in a family with a chemically dependent, mentally ill, or abusive parent, you ought to know how hard it is to display normalcy. You acknowledge that everyone in the family is affected. You either conform to the norm or reject it.

Over time, the family begins to revolve around maintaining the status quo, "the dysfunction." Now, the educator steps in. Rigid family rules and roles develop in the starving families. Hungry for attention or control. Maintaining this mindset allows the family's addict to keep using or the abuser to keep abusing. Understanding some of the rules that dominate dysfunctional families will help you escape these patterns. The educator encourages you to rebuild your self-esteem and form healthier relationships.

Control, fear, conflict, and abuse may have been ever present within your family makeup. The control element is disturbing. The abuser or molester lowers the victim's self-esteem and confidence by instilling fear. Since dependency was created when you try to break free, you feel increasing levels of withdrawal. At times, you may even feel worthless. But we must recognize that the abuse itself is an emotional rejection and that is why you are feeling abandoned.

Triggers of shame and fear are both present. The leading motive for someone to feed on other's fear by controlling them is selfish and twisted desires. You are not to blame, no matter how much they accuse you of deserving it. They twist the truth in order to control and manipulate you. You are blameless in your situation, though you were blamed. You were pure in your thoughts, but they polluted that purity. You didn't deserve any of it, but they convinced you that you deserved all of it. They tore you down to build themselves up.

Why does abusers do this? Why do they abuse? The fact is that they feel powerless and by stripping the power from someone else, it makes them feel powerful. They are insecure but may not show it. They use bullying and scare tactics to cover up the truth. In fact, often they turn into the bully after getting bullied themselves. We are all familiar with the truism "hurt people, hurt people." The one thing they all have in common is that their motive is to have power over their victim. You must not give them your power. They lack in areas of their own life, irrespective of worldly success. Therefore, they want to control you. Communication is a competition they must always be in the lead and win. Overcoming these types of attacks often go unnoticed. Seeking guidance from an educator or counselor can help encourage you in your darkest moments.

Emotional abuse is insidious. It will slowly eat away at your confidence and leave your self-esteem hanging in the balance. It often makes you put your worth into question. These demonic attacks forge suicide or homicide. Having people in your corner to help talk you off that cliff is crucial. You *are* worth it! An educator can be an excellent source to help you push forward. They will not judge you, but instead give you tools and advice to help you deal with your current and past situations. They have resources that can help you become the best version of yourself, while healing in the process.

> **If someone is going down the wrong road, he doesn't need motivation to speed him up. What he needs is education to turn him around.**
> *— Jim Rohn*

Do you recognize any of these characteristics within yourself or do you suffer from any of the conditions listed below? They are nothing to be ashamed of, but recognizing your issues is the first step in mending your brokenness. If you identify with any of these, an educator can confidentially assist you with the proper resources to put you on the path to healing.

- ⇒ Pessimism
- ⇒ Hypersensitivity
- ⇒ Easily angered
- ⇒ Negative mindset
- ⇒ Hopelessness
- ⇒ Insecurity
- ⇒ Jealousy
- ⇒ Aggressive behavior
- ⇒ Lashing out
- ⇒ Unable to concentrate
- ⇒ Victim mentality
- ⇒ Depression
- ⇒ Bipolarism
- ⇒ Schizophrenia
- ⇒ Personality disorders
- ⇒ Suicidal behavior

Until proper channels are set in place, the educator may advise you to protect your mind and heart. Though the absence of your father, bullying of peers, or an alcoholic mother may be ever so present, just know that these situations will pass. Don't let it kill the love that you have left in you. Though you may feel dead, you are very much alive. Surrounding yourself with people that will uplift you will help repair your mangled spirit.

The deeper you dive into discovering yourself, the more questions you will have. Your breath will become shallow indeed since life can present itself as a blank state of uncertainty. There's a mundane and motionless pit of absent thoughts of possibilities for success in a society designed full of hypocrites and opportunists. Feeling that this world was meant to demolish you just became real, but you feel that there's no escape. So, it leaves that burning question of... *why*? Why are you here? What's your purpose in life? Why have you gone through so much pain? Why are you given pleasures and opportunities just to have them ripped from you? These questions will be ongoing. That is perfectly normal. Working through them and finding answers are most important in finding yourself. The key is to not beat yourself up about it, but instead, explore possible ways to deal with your emotions. You may be surprised at how wise and strong you truly are.

Investment

Ever bought a cheap appliance, only to replace it a year later because its low price reflected its low quality? Ever tried to save money by staying in an inexpensive hotel? Only to find out management maintained the low prices to avoid investing in bug extermination. Now you are itching. Some of the best things are priced high for they are worth it. Forgiveness is placed in the "high-priced" category and some of us don't want to pay that cost. However, if you don't want to pay by constantly mending and fixing relationships in the future, you must swallow your pride and pay the price now. This goes for self-forgiveness as well.

If you are selfish with whom and how you show forgiveness, you will drip it out like a leaking faucet and your sink will never fill (you will not feel fulfilled). But if you turn it on full blast, holding back nothing, not only will you feel a resounding relief, but you will also have a sink full of fresh water. Sure, your water bill may be more costly, but you will pay the same amount over time with slow drips, and it will be painstakingly difficult to get a cup of water to quench your thirst.

Forgiveness is one of the deposits into life's bank, but adding benefit is also a great investment in any relationship. You have allowed people to cross the threshold of your life,

> **An investment in self-development pays the highest dividends."** –Debasish Mridha

but what was their investment worth? What was brought to the table for you? Ask yourself was it a good or bad investment for your life? What are you investing in others?

Steven invested all his trust in his wife. She was the center of his life and his confidant. He took a vow to love and protect her unconditionally, but these vows were put to the ultimate test. No one visualizes temptation, lust, distrust, and dishonor to sneak into their marriage, so if it does, it is appalling. Many marriages have been repaired after infidelities, but how? I'd imagine it's harder if your spouse cheats with someone you know. This was the case with Steven.

Steven and his brother were as thick as thieves. They told each other everything, but his brother did not relinquish having an affair with his wife. Life is not a movie, and no one wants to share or address the bad. Unambiguously, the vow was broken along with his heart. Witnessing it with his own two eyes, the pair could no longer deny it. He had a front row seat view to the master bedroom. The mirror on the wall reflected into the room and it was a reflection that he wished he hadn't seen. His bedroom was supposed to be a sacred place for him and his wife, but he was now living in a nightmare that he wished he could awaken from. Both his wife and his brother violated all love and respect they had for him. He felt the blood heating through his veins like a fire. His nostrils flared like a raging bull as his heart beat a million times a second. His hurt and disappointment turned into rage within a matter of seconds. Infuriated he was ready to kill.

He visualized slaying his brother right where he laid. Blood splatter across the white sheets that he and his wife picked out not too long ago. Steven and his brother had both been in the military. Their motto between themselves and to their country was always, "Death before dishonor." His brother dishonored him, and he felt like he needed to pay with his life. He ran through all the possible ways to hurt him. He exposed himself to ungodly ideas that would lead him (and them) down a deathly path. So, he stood there with tears in his eyes. Should he forgive his wife or bury them both? This moment instantly destroyed the healthiest relationships he thought he had. Now it was time to decide. Forgive, or do the unforgiveable. Steven's heart was too big to commit an act of crime, so he chose to forgive.

This road to forgiveness wasn't easy. There were substantial insecurities in his mind and his wall was up. For better and for worse had no room to maneuver and removing his brother from his life for the time being was crucial.

On this journey to forgiveness, Steven worried about working on and rediscovering himself instead of fixing his wife. He grew his faith and spirituality. In the process, his wife began assessing the rest of her relationships. She discovered that she was the problem in their marriage, not Steven. Her shortcomings had nothing to do with him, but they were merely selfish motives that boosted her self-esteem. Both Steven and his wife slowly formed a closer connection with God, which produced a new level of stability. This connection reinvigorated a newfound, healthy relationship.

She admitted to Steven how her low self-esteem was her ultimate, downfall. It was breathtaking for him to witness her growth as she learned how to value and love herself the way he always did. He could see her confidence evolving, as she started greeting him with a genuine smile on her face and love in her heart. She went from having mental breakdowns and anxiety attacks to pushing beyond her struggles by discovering true happiness.

Although Steven's situation could have drained and emptied him without any possibility of trusting her again, these burdens and fears did not stop him from living life. He learned to let go of the demons of doubt, took the gamble by giving her a second chance, and lifted the anchors of anger from his heart. He learned to love her again and to truly forgive. He learned more about how big he was as a person by paying the "high-price" for forgiveness than succumbing to pain and anger. That was the biggest flex of them all.

Value and worth are those things healthy marriages, strong families, soul-stirring churches, real friendships, and harmonious working environments thrive from. Relationships are cultivated and connections are airtight when the investments are commendable. Be sure that you are only depositing worthy relationships in your life. Anything less than that can amount in deficit of the mind and soul.

Empowerment

Strength and confidence grant an undeniable certainty and control over your life. In order to foster this power, you must first start with honesty and truthfulness within yourself. These magnets allow you to drag others to you for guidance, judgment, and advice. The magnet of guidance simply means you are the first line of defense. You tend to take chances that others fear, and you boldly speak about hard and unpleasant topics. The magnet of judgment allows you to see and feel situations that are hazardous then control them. The magnet of advice is of true concern and sound mind. You will identify a problem quietly and form a solution to rectify it.

Feeling empowered to be a magnet and make good decisions keeps you from jeopardizing your wellbeing and having blurred feelings. However, confidence should not be confused with cockiness. A confident man will reasonably accept the truth, no matter how tough it can be, and it won't hurt his manhood. He will own the truth, learn from it, and use it to better himself. Contrarily, a cocky man leads with his manhood and rejects the truth if it brings embarrassment, shame, or forces him to face his shortcomings. Evading the truth can move you to a lower level of emotion. Being true to yourself and others provides growth and builds character.

RESTORED

Life is a continual battle. We are in a constant state of regulating our emotions according to circumstance and environment. Even compassion, the concern we feel for another being's welfare, is sometimes treated with downright derision. Life often offers us weak and misguided sentiments, but you can always find strength through the wreckage. Even when there's no one else to comfort you, God's compassion can restore you, but you must also put in the work.

Sometimes, the expected comfort from people has the potential to mimic a shattered dream. Forgiveness is a moderate commodity, and most people avoid this entanglement of openness. What you need to realize is that God has already forgiven you. Now, it is your obligation to extend the same forgives to yourself and others. Yes, she wronged you. He did too. Maybe, all of them set out to attack you. But remember you weren't always right, yet you were forgiven during your time of iniquity.

> When I was a child, I spoke as a child, I understood as a child, I thought as a child; but when I became a man, I put away childish things.
> – 1 Corinthians 13:11

Forgiving those binding you in this entrenchment will transition you from the boy inside to the man that you are called to be. In your stunted stage, you were unaware of how to grow. You were deprived of necessary seeds and germination could not take place. Your inner struggles have made your garden dry up and now you are desperate for water or any type of nutrition. You have to feed your mind; you have to nourish your soul.

Now that this knowledge is at your fingertips, what will you do with it? You've heard the cliché "history is bound to repeat itself," but the notion failed to mention that delayed obedience is disobedience. You need to act on tending to yourself in order to seek healing. If you allow guilt, anger, and depression to manifest, you will be filled with cancerous, festering grudges toward the people you loved.

Don't get it wrong, people must be made aware of the hurt they inflict on you. Forgiving them allows the repairing of a damaged vessel created by egregious acts to be noticed. Forgiveness and restoration together are a consummate mission. Consider each of the lily pads of destruction that you used as steppingstones. Each time you placed your foot on them, you sank. Your burdens were too heavy. But with forgiveness and restoration, you will be light, and those old hidden struggles will not feel as heavy as before.

Taking time to pray, self-reflect, analyze, and process situations are all critical elements for your growth. It is necessary to spend a little time each day reflecting or meditating. Stop searching for excuses to stay in a stagnant, hopeless, hurtful place.

It's time to arrive to the place of healing. You can do this by identifying issues affecting you and seeking counsel for better understanding and clarity. In life we are forever learning. You must learn to adjust and be flexible as time go on. You'll notice that hurdles that were too high to clear will become an ease to jump. You will be able to brush off things that used to aggravate you. You will learn to walk away from people and situations that no longer serve you. You *will* be a conqueror.

Now you have arrived. You are at a place that will require you to forgive yourself for holding on to that stuff so long. Are you ready to let it go? Are you there yet? It's your time. It's time that you are restored. Dig yourself from the trenches, dust yourself off and shine. You are valuable. You are no longer a broken gem.